UX FOR ECOMMERCE

A Comprehensive Guide to Improve Your Online Store and Drive Sales

FABRIZIO MICHELS

Contents

I would like to express my gratitude to my wife and family for their unwavering patience and support during the course of my work on this book.

Thank you!

Who This Book is For

This book is for anyone who owns or operates an online store and wants to improve their user experience and drive sales. This includes business owners, eCommerce managers, marketers, web developers, UX designers, and anyone else involved in creating or managing an online store. The book provides a comprehensive overview of UX principles and strategies specific to eCommerce, covering topics such as user journey mapping, visual design and branding, prototyping, usability testing, and interaction design. It is suitable for both beginners and experienced professionals in the eCommerce industry who want to improve their online store's user experience and overall performance.

Why I Wrote This Book

As someone who has spent their career working with eCommerce websites in various capacities, including as a designer, developer, marketing director, and owner, I have developed a deep understanding of user behavior and preferences. Utilizing this knowledge, I strive to create engaging and intuitive experiences for online shoppers. My extensive experience in the industry led me to write a book on UX for eCommerce with the goal of sharing my insights and strategies with others who are looking to improve their online store's user experience.

This comprehensive guide offers practical tips and advice on designing effective interfaces, improving site navigation, creating compelling visual designs, and optimizing the checkout process. I believe that my unique perspective can be particularly valuable in addressing both the creative and technical aspects of UX design for eCommerce. Ultimately, my hope is that this book can assist you in creating visually appealing, user-friendly, and sales-optimized online stores.

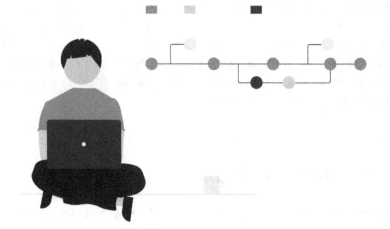

Chapter 1: Understanding the Importance of User Experience (UX) in Online Stores

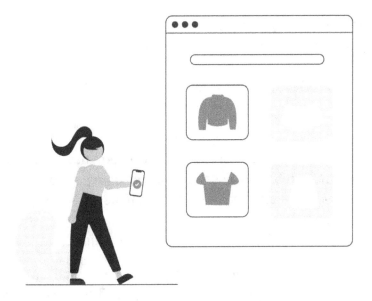

The basics of UX and its impact on online stores

User experience (UX) is the process of designing and creating user-friendly interfaces that improve the overall experience for users. It involves creating intuitive and easy-to-use interfaces that make it easy for users to interact with products or services.

UX refers to the overall experience a user has when interacting with a product, system, or service. In the context of online stores, UX design refers to the experience a customer has when visiting an online store and trying to complete a purchase.

A good UX design can have a significant impact on online stores by increasing customer satisfaction, loyalty, and sales.

UX Design tools and how they impact online stores:

- **User research**: Understanding users' needs, behaviors, and motivations is essential to designing an online store that meets their needs and expectations. User research can help identify pain points in the user journey, which can be addressed through design improvements.

- **Information architecture**: A clear and well-organized information architecture can make it easier for users to find what they are looking for in an online store, leading to improved user engagement and conversion rates.

- **User journey mapping**: Mapping out the user journey can identify areas where users may be experiencing frustration or confusion, which can be addressed through design improvements to increase user engagement and conversion rates.

- **Wireframing**: Wireframing is an essential step in designing an online store's layout and functionality. By testing and refining design concepts, wireframing can help create a more engaging and user-friendly online store.

- **Visual design**: The visual design of an online store can impact users' perceptions of the store's credibility, professionalism, and trustworthiness. A well-designed visual interface can increase user engagement and conversion rates.

- **Prototyping**: Prototyping allows designers to test and validate design decisions before launching an online store. This can help identify and address usability issues, leading to increased engagement and conversion rates.

- **Responsive design**: Responsive design is essential to ensuring that an online store works well on all devices, which can improve user engagement and conversion rates by accommodating users' preferred device types.

- **Usability testing:** Conducting usability testing on an online store can identify areas for improvement in the user experience, leading to increased engagement and conversion rates.

- **Interaction design**: A well-designed interaction design can make it easier for users to navigate an online store and complete their desired actions, such as making a purchase or signing up for a newsletter.

- **Accessibility**: Designing for accessibility can increase the usability of an online store for users with disabilities, which can broaden the store's customer base and improve its reputation as an inclusive and socially responsible brand.

The impact of UX on online stores can be significant, actually, UX design plays a crucial role in the success of online stores. A well-designed and user-friendly online store can improve customer satisfaction and drive sales. In contrast, a poorly designed online store can frustrate users and drive them away from the website. By focusing on the basics of UX, online stores can create interfaces that are easy to use and appealing to their target audience, which in turn can lead to increased sales and customer loyalty.

The role of UX in increasing user engagement and conversion rates

The user experience (UX) plays a critical role in increasing user engagement and conversion rates. UX refers to the overall experience that users have when interacting with a product or service, including how easy it is to use, how intuitive the interface is, and how well it meets the user's needs and expectations.

When it comes to increasing user engagement, UX can make a big difference. A well-designed user experience can help users stay on a website or app longer, making it more likely that they will engage with the content, products, or services offered. This can lead to higher conversion rates, as users are more likely to take the desired action, such as making a purchase or signing up for a newsletter.

There are many ways that UX can increase user engagement and conversion rates:

- **Simplify the user interface**: By making the user interface simple and intuitive, users can quickly find what they are looking for, reducing frustration and increasing engagement.

- **Clear and simple navigation**: A clear and simple navigation system helps users find what they are looking for quickly and easily. This makes it more likely that they will engage with the website and ultimately make a purchase.

- **Improve website speed**: Slow-loading websites can be a major turnoff for users, leading to high bounce rates and decreased engagement. Improving website speed can increase user engagement and reduce bounce rates.

- **Use clear and concise language:** Using clear and concise language can improve the user experience by reducing confusion and frustration. Users are more likely to engage with a website and convert when the language is easy to understand.

- **Provide clear calls-to-action (CTAs)**: A clear and prominent CTA can encourage users to take action, whether it is to make a purchase, sign up for a newsletter, or download a resource.

- **Optimize the checkout process**: A complex or confusing checkout process can lead to high cart abandonment rates. By optimizing the checkout process and making it easy for users to complete their purchase, conversion rates can be improved.

- **Use high-quality images and videos**: High-quality visuals can increase user engagement by making the website more visually appealing and conveying information more effectively.

- **Incorporate social proof**: Using social proof, such as customer reviews and ratings, can increase user trust in the website and encourage them to engage and convert.

- **Customer reviews and ratings**: Including customer reviews and ratings can increase user engagement and trust in the website, as users can see what others have thought of the products they are interested in.

- **Personalize the user experience**: Personalizing the user experience can make users feel valued and increase engagement. This can be achieved through personalized recommendations, targeted content, and customized messaging.

Why UX is essential for building brand loyalty and customer satisfaction

User experience (UX) is essential for building brand loyalty and customer satisfaction because it is the foundation for creating positive and memorable interactions between a user and a product or service. When users have a great experience with a brand, they are more likely to return and become loyal customers. Here are a few reasons why UX is so important for building brand loyalty and customer satisfaction:

There are several reasons why UX is so important for building brand loyalty and customer satisfaction:

User-centric design

UX focuses on designing products and services with the end user in mind. By prioritizing the needs and preferences of users, designers can create a more user-friendly and enjoyable experience, which can lead to increased satisfaction and loyalty.

Ease of use

A good UX design can make it easier for customers to find what they are looking for, complete their desired actions, and navigate the product or service. This can result in increased satisfaction and loyalty, as customers are more likely to use a product or service that is easy and enjoyable to use.

Consistency

Consistency in UX design can help build trust and familiarity with a brand. When users know what to expect and are able to rely on a consistent experience, they are more likely to continue using the product or service and recommend it to others.

Emotional connection

A well-designed UX can create an emotional connection with customers by providing a positive and memorable experience. This emotional connection can lead to increased brand loyalty and customer satisfaction.

Reduced frustration

A frustrating user experience can lead to dissatisfaction and ultimately, disloyalty. UX design can help reduce frustration by simplifying complex processes, providing clear instructions and feedback, and ensuring that the product or service meets user needs.

Increased engagement

A good UX design can increase user engagement by creating a more immersive and interactive experience. This can lead to increased satisfaction and loyalty, as users are more likely to continue using a product or service that they enjoy and find engaging.

Competitive advantage

In today's highly competitive marketplace, a well-designed UX can help set a brand apart from its competitors. By providing a better user experience, brands can attract and retain customers, leading to increased loyalty and satisfaction.

By prioritizing UX design, brands can create a more user-friendly and enjoyable experience for their customers, leading to increased satisfaction, loyalty, and ultimately, business success.

Summary

UX is the process of creating user-friendly interfaces that enhance the overall user experience. In the context of online stores, UX design involves improving the experience customers have when trying to purchase a product.

Good UX design can significantly improve customer satisfaction, loyalty, and sales. UX plays a critical role in increasing user engagement and conversion rates by simplifying the interface, improving website speed, using clear language, providing clear calls-to-action, optimizing the checkout process, using high-quality images and videos, incorporating social proof, and personalizing the user experience. Finally, UX is essential for building brand loyalty and customer satisfaction by creating positive and memorable experiences for users.

Chapter 2: User Research and Analysis

User research and analysis is important for an online store because it helps to understand the needs, preferences, and behaviors of users. By understanding the user, online stores can create a user experience that is tailored to their target audience, resulting in higher conversion rates, customer satisfaction, and loyalty.

UX Research Objectives

The objectives of UX research can vary depending on the specific project, but here are some common objectives that online stores may have when conducting UX research:

- **Understand user needs**: UX research can help stores gain a better understanding of their target audience's needs, preferences, and behaviors when interacting with a product.

- **Identify pain points**: By observing and collecting feedback from users, businesses can identify pain points in the user experience that need to be addressed to improve overall satisfaction.

- **Improve usability:** UX research can help identify areas where usability can be improved, such as by streamlining workflows, simplifying navigation, or improving the clarity of instructions or feedback.

- **Enhance user engagement:** UX research can help identify features or design elements that will increase user engagement and encourage users to interact more with the product or service.

- **Increase conversions**: UX research can help identify barriers to conversion, such as confusing or lengthy checkout processes, and suggest improvements to increase conversion rates.

- **Validate design decisions**: UX research can help validate design decisions by testing prototypes or mockups with users to ensure they meet user needs and preferences.

- **Benchmark performance**: UX research can be used to benchmark performance against competitors or previous versions of the product or service, identifying areas for improvement and tracking progress over time.

TAKE ACTION
Use UX Research to understand user needs and identify pain points

1. Define your goals
2. Identify the research question
3. Select Research Methods
4. Recruit Participants
5. Create the research materials
6. Conduct Research
7. Analyze Data
8. Draw conclusions
9. Share the findings

1. Define your goals

Start by identifying what you want to achieve through UX research. Are you looking to increase sales, improve user satisfaction, or reduce cart abandonment rates? Defining your goals will help you focus your research efforts and identify the right metrics to measure success.

2. Identify the research question

Try to identify the research question or problem you want to solve. This will help guide the research and ensure you collect the relevant information.

3. Select Research Methods

Choose the appropriate research methods to gather information about user needs. There are several UX research methods that can be used to gather insights about user needs, behaviors, and attitudes. Here are some of the most common methods:

- **Surveys**: Surveys are a cost-effective way to gather feedback from a large number of users. Surveys can be administered online or in-person and can provide insights into user preferences, satisfaction levels, and pain points.

- **Interviews**: Interviews are a more in-depth method of gathering feedback from users. Interviews can be conducted in-person, over the phone, or online, and can provide deeper insights into user motivations, behaviors, and attitudes.

- **Focus groups**: Focus groups involve bringing together a small group of users to discuss a specific topic or product. Focus groups can provide valuable insights into user opinions, preferences, and attitudes, as well as identify pain points and areas for improvement.

- **Usability testing**: Usability testing involves observing users as they interact with a product or website to identify areas where they experience difficulties or confusion. Usability testing can be conducted in-person or remotely and can help identify usability issues that can be addressed to improve the user experience.

- **A/B testing**: A/B testing involves testing two versions of a product or website to determine which version performs better in terms of user engagement or conversion rates. A/B testing can help identify which design elements or features are most effective in meeting user needs.

- **Card sorting**: Card sorting involves asking users to organize items or features into groups, which can help inform the structure and organization of a website or product.

- **Diary studies**: Diary studies involve asking users to record their experiences using a product or website over a period of time. Diary studies can provide insights into user behaviors, motivations, and pain points over an extended period.

By using one or a combination of these methods, businesses can gain valuable insights into user needs and preferences, which can be used to improve the user experience and drive business success.

4. Recruit Participants

Recruit participants who are representative of your target audience to ensure that the feedback you receive is relevant and actionable. You can recruit participants through social media, email campaigns, or online communities.

5. Create the research materials

Design the research materials such as interview questions, survey questions, or tasks for usability testing. Ensure that the questions are clear and unbiased.

6. Conduct Research

Use the selected research methods to gather data about user needs. For example, you might conduct interviews to gain a deeper understanding of user motivations or run surveys to gather feedback on specific features.

7. Analyze Data

Once you have collected data, analyze it to identify common themes and patterns. Look for areas where users express frustration or confusion, as well as areas where they express satisfaction or enthusiasm.

To effectively analyze data from UX (User Experience) research and improve an online store, you can follow these steps:

- **Identify patterns and trends**: Look for patterns and trends in the data that can help you identify common themes and areas for improvement. For example, you might notice that users are struggling to find specific products, or that they are frustrated with a particular aspect of the checkout process.

- **Categorize feedback**: Categorize feedback based on the type of feedback received. For example, you might categorize feedback as positive, negative, or neutral, or categorize feedback based on the specific aspect of the website being reviewed.

- **Prioritize issues:** Prioritize the issues based on their impact on the user experience and their potential for improvement.

Focus on addressing issues that have the greatest impact on user satisfaction, engagement, and conversion rates.

- **Identify root causes**: Look for the root causes of usability issues, rather than just addressing the symptoms. For example, if users are struggling to find specific products, the root cause might be poor search functionality or a confusing navigation structure.

- **Make data-driven decisions**: Use the insights gained from your UX research to make data-driven decisions about how to improve the user experience. For example, you might decide to redesign the search functionality or streamline the checkout process based on user feedback.

- **Test and iterate**: Test your design changes with users and iterate based on their feedback. Continuously test and improve to ensure that your online store is meeting the needs of your users and driving business success.

8. Draw conclusions

Draw conclusions based on the data collected, and use the insights to inform design decisions.

9. Share the findings

Share the findings with stakeholders, designers, and developers. Communicate the insights in a clear and concise manner, and make recommendations for design improvements based on the research findings.

Tools for UX Research

There are several tools available to help you with your UX Research project. Here are some examples:

1. **Google Analytics**: a web analytics service that provides valuable insights into user behavior on your website.

2. **Hotjar**: a tool that provides heat maps, session recordings, and surveys to help you understand how users interact with your website.

3. **Optimal Workshop**: a suite of tools for user research, including card sorting, tree testing, and surveys.

4. **Usabilla**: a platform that allows you to collect user feedback through surveys, feedback widgets, and in-page feedback tools.

5. **Ethnio**: a tool that helps you recruit participants for user research studies, including usability testing and surveys.

6. **SurveyMonkey**: a tool that allows you to create and distribute surveys to gather user feedback.

7. **Qualtrics**: a tool that provides advanced survey and data analysis capabilities for user research studies.

Create User Personas

Use the insights gained from your research to create user personas, which are fictional representations of your typical users. Personas can help you keep the needs of your users at the forefront of your design decisions and ensure that you are designing with their needs in mind. Creating user personas is important for an online store because it helps to develop a deeper understanding of the target audience, their needs, and behaviors.

Creating a user persona for an online store can be a simple and effective way to gain a deeper understanding of the target audience. Here are the basic steps to create a user persona:

1. **Identify common characteristics**: Review the data and identify common characteristics among the target audience. For example, you might notice that the target audience is primarily young professionals who are interested in eco-friendly products.

2. **Create a profile**: Use the common characteristics to create a profile of the ideal customer. Give the user persona a name and create a detailed description of their background, goals, challenges, and behaviors. Use the information you have gathered to make the persona as realistic as possible.

3. **Add a photo**: To make the user persona more tangible, add a photo or illustration that represents the persona. This can help you to visualize the persona as a real person and make it easier to communicate the persona to others.

4. **Use the persona**: Once you have created the user persona, use it to guide your design and marketing decisions. Consider how the persona would interact with your online store and use their goals and behaviors to inform your design decisions.

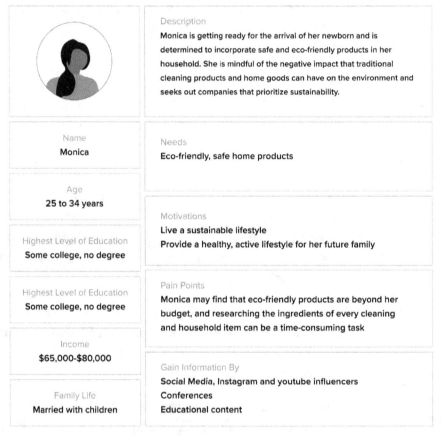

Description

Monica is getting ready for the arrival of her newborn and is determined to incorporate safe and eco-friendly products in her household. She is mindful of the negative impact that traditional cleaning products and home goods can have on the environment and seeks out companies that prioritize sustainability.

Name
Monica

Needs
Eco-friendly, safe home products

Age
25 to 34 years

Motivations
Live a sustainable lifestyle
Provide a healthy, active lifestyle for her future family

Highest Level of Education
Some college, no degree

Pain Points
Monica may find that eco-friendly products are beyond her budget, and researching the ingredients of every cleaning and household item can be a time-consuming task

Highest Level of Education
Some college, no degree

Income
$65,000-$80,000

Gain Information By
Social Media, Instagram and youtube influencers
Conferences
Educational content

Family Life
Married with children

Fig 2.1: Persona Example Template

User Personas and Marketing

Later you can use your user personas to help marketing your online store or product. User personas provide a deep understanding of the target audience that can help marketing teams to create more effective campaigns, improve segmentation, and drive customer acquisition and retention.

Targeted messaging

User personas provide a deep understanding of the target audience, including their needs, behaviors, and pain points. This understanding can help marketing teams to craft targeted messaging that speaks to the specific needs and interests of the target audience. By speaking directly to the target audience, marketing messages are more likely to resonate with potential customers and lead to higher conversion rates.

Tailored campaigns

User personas can also help marketing teams to create tailored campaigns that speak to specific user groups. For example, if the online store targets both young adults and seniors, user personas can help to identify the differences in their preferences and behaviors, and tailor the marketing campaigns accordingly. This can result in a more effective marketing campaign that leads to higher engagement and sales.

Better segmentation

User personas can also help marketing teams to segment their audience more effectively. By identifying different user groups with different needs and behaviors, marketing teams can create targeted campaigns that speak directly to those groups. This can result in a more efficient use of marketing resources and higher conversion rates.

Using UX Research to improve usability

When it comes to eCommerce, the objectives of UX research can be particularly important in terms of driving sales, improving user satisfaction, and increasing customer loyalty. Below are some ways to use UX research to improve the usability and overall experience of your online store:

Optimize product page design

UX research can help optimize product page design to ensure that users have all the information they need to make a purchase decision, such as high-quality images, clear product descriptions, and customer reviews.

Streamline checkout process

UX research can help identify areas where the checkout process can be streamlined to reduce friction and increase completion rates, such as by minimizing the number of steps or improving the clarity of instructions.

Improve search functionality

UX research can help identify ways to improve search functionality, such as by refining search algorithms or offering advanced filtering options.

Improve website navigation

Navigation is key to helping users find what they're looking for quickly and easily. UX research can help identify areas where navigation can be improved, such as through clearer labeling or more intuitive menu structures.

Enhance mobile experience

With more users shopping on mobile devices, UX research can help identify ways to improve the mobile user experience, such as by optimizing page load times or simplifying navigation.

Personalize the user experience

UX research can help identify user preferences and behaviors, allowing businesses to personalize the user experience by offering tailored product recommendations or targeted promotions.

Increase customer loyalty

UX research can help identify areas where the user experience can be improved to increase customer loyalty, such as by offering a seamless omnichannel experience or providing excellent customer support.

"Research is to see what everybody else has seen, and to think what nobody else has thought."

- Albert Szent-Gyorgyi

Chapter 3: Information Architecture

Information architecture is crucial for online stores, as it helps users navigate the website and find what they are looking for quickly and easily. Let's have a look at some of the best strategies for information architecture in online stores:

Create Clear Categories

Create clear and concise categories for your products that make sense to your users. Use common and familiar terms for your categories, and avoid industry jargon that might be confusing.

Analyze Content

Analyze the existing content on your online store and categorize it based on its relevance to your target audience. For example, you can group products into categories, such as electronics, clothing, or beauty.

Use a Logical Hierarchy

A logical hierarchy is essential for organizing your products in a way that makes sense to users. Group similar products together and create subcategories as needed to create a hierarchy that users can easily understand and navigate.

Provide Effective Navigation

Provide clear and easy-to-use navigation menus that allow users to quickly find the products they are looking for. Consider using mega-menus, dropdown menus, or breadcrumb navigation to help users move through your site.

Use Product Filters

Using product filters allows users to refine their search results and find exactly what they are looking for. Consider providing filters for price, size, color, and other relevant attributes to help users narrow down their search results.

Provide Product Recommendations

Providing product recommendations can help users discover new products and increase the likelihood of making a purchase. Use algorithms to recommend products based on user behavior and search history.

Overall, effective information architecture is essential for creating a positive user experience on an online store. By conducting user research, creating clear categories, implementing logical hierarchy, providing effective navigation, implementing search functionality, using product filters, and providing product recommendations, you can help users find what they need quickly and easily, leading to increased sales and customer satisfaction.

Usability and Navigation

Usability and navigation are critical for an online store because they play a key role in the overall user experience, which can have a significant impact on conversion rates and customer satisfaction. Here are some reasons why usability and navigation are so important for an online store:

They can make or break the first impression

When users visit an online store, their first impression is critical. If the website is difficult to navigate or the user experience is poor, users are likely to become frustrated and leave the website. On the other hand, if the website is easy to use and navigate, users are more likely to have a positive impression and continue exploring the website.

They can affect conversion rates

The Navigation of an online store can have a direct impact on conversion rates. If the checkout process is confusing or difficult to use, users are more likely to abandon their cart and not complete their purchase. However, if the checkout process is streamlined and user-friendly, users are more likely to complete their purchase and become repeat customers.

They can impact customer satisfaction

Usability and navigation can also impact customer satisfaction. If users have a difficult time finding what they are looking for or navigating the website, they are likely to become frustrated and have a negative experience. On the other hand, if the website is easy to use and navigate, users are more likely to have a positive experience and become repeat customers.

Designing Intuitive And Easy-To-Use Navigation For Online Stores

Designing intuitive and easy-to-use navigation is crucial for online stores as it directly affects the user experience of the customers. If the navigation of an online store is poorly designed, it can be frustrating for users to find the products they are looking for, leading to a high bounce rate and a decrease in sales. A well-designed navigation system should be clear, concise, and easy to understand, making it easy for users to navigate through the website and find what they need quickly. Additionally, a good navigation system should allow users to filter and sort products based on their preferences, making the shopping experience more personalized and enjoyable.

Another important aspect of designing intuitive and easy-to-use navigation for online stores is that it can increase customer loyalty and retention. If customers have a positive experience while navigating through an online store, they are more likely to return to the website in the future and make repeat purchases. A well-designed navigation system can also help build trust and credibility with customers, as it shows that the online store is organized and professional. Ultimately, an intuitive and easy-to-use navigation system is critical for online stores as it directly impacts the user experience, sales, and customer loyalty.

TAKE ACTION
Design intuitive and easy-to-use navigation for your project
1. Make it simple
2. Use clear and descriptive labels
3. Make it consistent
4. Optimize for mobile devices:
5. Use visual cues
6. Test and iterate

1. Make it simple

Simple navigation is easier for users to understand and navigate. Limit the number of main menu items and avoid cluttering the navigation bar with too many sub-menus.

2. Use clear and descriptive labels

Use labels that accurately describe the content that users will find when they click on a link. Avoid vague or unclear labels that can confuse users.

3. Make it consistent

Keep the navigation consistent across the entire website, including the layout, language, and formatting. Users should always know where they are and how to get back to the main navigation menu.

4. Optimize for mobile devices

Mobile devices account for a significant portion of online shopping, so it is essential to design navigation that is optimized for smaller screens. Use responsive design techniques to ensure that the navigation is easy to use on all devices.

5. Use visual cues

Visual cues can help guide users through the navigation and make it easier to understand. Use icons, images, or other visual cues to help users quickly identify menu items.

6. Test and iterate

User testing is essential for determining how users interact with the navigation and identifying areas that can be improved. Test the navigation with a sample of users and iterate based on their feedback.

Content Strategy

The best strategy for content creation and information architecture of an online store involves understanding the target audience and creating content that is relevant, engaging, and easy to navigate.

There are some key considerations for creating an effective content strategy and information architecture for an online store:

- **Understand the target audience**: Before creating content, it's important to understand the target audience and their needs, interests, and preferences. This can be done through user research, surveys, and analytics data.

- **Define the content goals**: The content goals should be aligned with the business goals of the online store. These goals may include increasing engagement, driving conversions, and building brand awareness.

- **Develop a content strategy**: The content strategy should be based on the target audience and the content goals. It should include the types of content to be created, the topics to be covered, and the frequency of content updates.

- **Create high-quality content**: The content should be high-quality, relevant, and engaging. It should be easy to read and visually appealing. The use of images, videos, and infographics can help to make the content more engaging.

- **Continuously evaluate and improve the content strategy**: The content strategy should be evaluated on a regular basis to determine its effectiveness. This can be done through analytics data and user feedback. The content strategy should be updated and improved based on these insights

.

Writing effective copy that engages users and promotes sales

Effective copywriting can play a crucial role in increasing sales for an online store. There are several ways that effective copy can make a difference. Firstly, it can grab the attention of potential customers and draw them into the product page by using attention-grabbing headlines, subheadings, and descriptions. Secondly, it can establish the value of the product, highlighting its features, benefits, and unique selling points by using persuasive language and providing clear, concise descriptions. Thirdly, it can build trust with customers by providing information about the product, such as its origin, ingredients, and manufacturing process, which can help establish the credibility of the online store and build trust with potential customers. Fourthly, it can create a sense of urgency and encourage customers to make a purchase by using limited-time offers, scarcity tactics, and persuasive language to encourage customers to act quickly. Lastly, it can encourage customers to take action by including clear calls to action, such as "Add to Cart" or "Buy Now," which can help increase conversion rates and drive sales. It's important to continually test and iterate copy to ensure that it resonates with your target audience and meets their needs and expectations.

Best practices for writing effective copy that engages users and promotes sales

Focus on benefits

Highlight the benefits of your products or services, and explain how they can solve the problems or meet the needs of your target audience.

Use clear and concise language

Write in a clear and simple language that is easy to understand, and avoid using jargon or technical terms that might confuse or alienate users.

Use persuasive language

Use persuasive language and calls-to-action to encourage users to take the desired action, such as making a purchase or subscribing to a newsletter.

Create a sense of urgency

Use time-limited offers, limited stock alerts, or other urgency-building tactics to create a sense of urgency and encourage users to take action quickly.

Use social proof

Use customer reviews, ratings, or testimonials to provide social proof and build trust with potential customers.

Test and refine

Use analytics and A/B testing to test the effectiveness of your copy, and make adjustments as needed.

SEO

SEO stands for Search Engine Optimization, which is the practice of optimizing websites and their content to increase their visibility and ranking in search engine results pages (SERPs). The goal of SEO is to increase organic traffic to a website from search engines by improving its relevance and authority for specific search queries.

Search engines like Google, Bing, and Yahoo use complex algorithms to determine which websites should appear in their search results for specific queries. These algorithms consider several factors, including the relevance of the content to the query, the quality and authority of the website, and the user experience of the website.

SEO includes a range of techniques, including keyword research, on-page optimization, link building, and technical optimization, to help websites rank higher in search results. By optimizing their website for SEO, businesses can increase their visibility in search engines and drive more traffic to their site.

SEO is important for an online store for several reasons:

- **Increased Visibility**: By optimizing an online store for search engines, it becomes more visible to potential customers who are actively searching for products or services similar to what the store offers. This increased visibility can lead to increased website traffic and sales.

- **Higher Ranking**: The higher an online store ranks in search engine results pages, the more likely potential customers are to click through to the site. By implementing SEO techniques such as keyword research and optimization, online stores can improve their ranking in search results, making them more visible to potential customers.

- **Competitive Advantage**: With so many online stores competing for the attention of potential customers, those that have invested in SEO will have an advantage over those that have not. Online stores that appear higher in search engine results pages are more likely to attract customers and generate sales.

- **Better User Experience:** Many of the techniques used in SEO, such as optimizing website speed, improving site structure and navigation, and creating high-quality content, also improve the user experience of an online store. A better user experience can lead to increased engagement, longer site visits, and increased customer loyalty.

- **Cost-Effective Marketing**: SEO can be a cost-effective marketing strategy for online stores, especially when compared to other forms of online advertising. Once an online store has optimized its website for SEO, it can continue to generate traffic and sales without ongoing advertising costs.

SEO Best Practises for an Online Store

1. **Keyword research**: Conduct thorough keyword research to understand the keywords and phrases potential customers are searching for in relation to the products you sell. Use this research to optimize your website content, including product descriptions, category pages, and blog posts.

2. **On-page optimization**: Optimize your website pages by including relevant keywords in titles, headings, meta descriptions, and content. Use schema markup to help search engines understand your website content and improve your visibility in search results.

3. **Mobile optimization**: Ensure that your online store is optimized for mobile devices. This includes having a responsive design that adapts to different screen sizes, optimizing page load times, and making sure your website is easy to navigate on a mobile device.

4. **Link building**: Build high-quality backlinks to your online store by creating content that other websites will want to link to. This can include blog posts, infographics, and other types of content that provide value to your audience.

5. **Social media**: Use social media to promote your online store and share your content. This can help increase visibility and drive traffic to your website.

6. **Local SEO**: If you have a physical store, use local SEO techniques to improve your visibility in local search results. This can include creating a Google My Business listing, optimizing your website for local keywords, and building local citations.

Chapter 4: User Journey Mapping

Understanding user behavior and the customer journey of an online store is critical for improving the user experience and increasing conversions.

User journey mapping is important for an online store because it helps businesses understand their customers' experience and behavior as they navigate through the website. By mapping out the user journey, online stores can identify pain points and areas where customers may get stuck or frustrated, as well as opportunities to improve the overall user experience.

User journey mapping involves creating a visual representation of the steps that a customer takes from initial awareness of the product or service to the final purchase decision. It helps online stores to see the big picture and identify opportunities to optimize the customer journey at every touchpoint.

By identifying pain points in the customer journey, online stores can make improvements to the website, such as simplifying the checkout process, making it easier to find relevant products, or providing more information about shipping and returns policies.

User journey mapping can also help online stores identify new opportunities to engage with customers throughout their journey.

Analyze Website Analytics

Website analytics tools can provide data on user behavior, such as bounce rates, time on site, and conversion rates. This data can help identify where users are dropping off in the customer journey and where improvements can be made.

Use Heatmaps And Click-Tracking

Heatmaps and click-tracking tools can help identify where users are clicking on the website and where they are spending the most time. This can help identify which areas of the website are the most engaging and which areas may need improvement.

Map Out The Customer Journey

Mapping out the customer journey can help identify touchpoints and interactions that users have with the online store. This can help identify areas where the user experience could be improved, such as by streamlining the checkout process or providing more detailed product information.

Creating a user journey map is a visual representation of the steps a user takes to achieve a goal on your website or application. Here are the steps to create a user journey map:

1. **Use your User Persona**: Start by identifying the specific user persona you are designing for. Consider their goals, motivations, pain points, and behaviors. This information will help you design a journey map that is tailored to your user's needs.. This helps you understand your users' goals, motivations, and pain points.

2. **Identify the User's Goal**: Identify the user's primary goal, such as making a purchase, signing up for a newsletter, or completing a form.

3. **Map Out the User Steps**: Map out the user journey from start to finish, including every step the user takes to achieve their goal. This may include visiting your website, browsing products, adding items to their cart, and completing the checkout process.

4. **Identify Touchpoints**: Identify all touchpoints the user interacts with during their journey, such as your website, mobile app, social media channels, customer service, and other relevant channels.

5. **Identify Pain Points and Opportunities:** Identify pain points the user experiences during their journey, such as slow page load times, confusing navigation, or unclear instructions. Also, identify opportunities to improve the user experience, such as providing helpful tips, personalized recommendations, or relevant content.

6. **Map Out Emotions**: Map out the emotions the user experiences during their journey. This helps you understand how your users feel at each stage of the journey and what triggers those emotions.

7. **Prioritize Improvements**: Prioritize improvements based on the pain points and opportunities identified during the user journey map. This helps you focus on the most significant areas for improvement and enhance the user experience.

STAGE	AWARENESS	CONSIDERATION	DECISION	SERVICE	LOYALTY
CUSTOMER ACTIONS	View online ad, social media campaign, hear about from friends	Conduct research, research competitors, compare features and pricing	Make a Purchase	Receive product, contact customer service, read product documentation	Make another purchase, share experience
TOUCHPOINTS	traditional media, social media, word of mouth	Word of mouth, website, social media	Website, mobile app or phone	Phone, email, chatbot	Word of mouth, review sites, social media
CUSTOMER EXPERIENCE/ EMOTIONS	Interested, hesitant 😐	Curious, excited 🙂	Happy & Excited 🙂	Frustrated 🙁	Satisfied, excited 😊
KPIS	Number of people reached	New website visitors	Conversion rate, online sales	Product reviews, customer service rate	Retention rate, customer satisfaction score
BUSINESS GOALS	Increase awareness, interest	Increase website visitors	Increase conversion rate, online sales	Increase customer service satisfaction	Generate positive reviews, increase retention rate

Fig 4.1: Customer Journey Map Example

Monitor And Adjust Continuously

Understanding user behavior and the customer journey is an ongoing process, and designers and developers should continuously monitor and adjust their approach based on user feedback and data.

Summary

Understanding user behavior and the customer journey is essential to improving the user experience and increasing conversions.

By conducting user research, analyzing website analytics, using heatmaps and click-tracking, mapping out the customer journey, gathering customer feedback, conducting A/B testing, and monitoring and adjusting continuously, designers and developers can gain valuable insights into how users are interacting with the online store and identify areas where improvements can be made to enhance the overall user experience.

Chapter 5: Wireframing

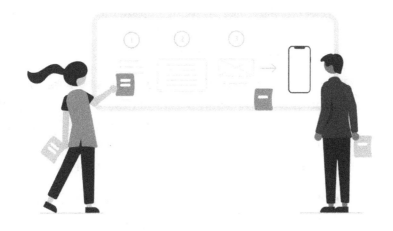

Wireframing and prototyping are essential steps in the process of building online stores that can save time and money by helping to identify and address design and usability issues early in the development process. Here are some ways wireframing and prototyping can save time and money when building online stores:

- **Identify and Address Design and Usability Issues Early**: Wireframing and prototyping allow you to identify and address design and usability issues early in the development process. This helps to reduce the time and cost of making changes later in the development cycle.

- **Test Different Design Approaches:** Wireframes and prototypes allow you to test different design approaches before committing to a final design. This can save time and money by helping you avoid costly mistakes and ensuring that the final design is effective and user-friendly.

- **Get Stakeholder Buy-In**: Wireframes and prototypes can be used to get stakeholder buy-in and ensure that everyone involved in the development process is on the same page. This can save time and money by reducing the likelihood of miscommunications and misunderstandings.

- **Reduce Development Time**: By identifying and addressing design and usability issues early in the development process, wireframing and prototyping can reduce the time it takes to build an online store. This can save money by reducing development costs and getting the store up and running faster.

- **Improve User Experience**: Wireframing and prototyping allow you to focus on the user experience and ensure that the online store is easy to use and navigate. This can lead to increased customer satisfaction and loyalty, which can ultimately drive sales and revenue

How to create a wireframe

There are several ways to create a wireframe for an online store, but the easiest way will depend on your personal preferences and familiarity with different tools:

Pen and Paper

One of the easiest and most straightforward ways to create a wireframe is to sketch it out with a pen and paper. This is a quick way to jot down your ideas and visualize the layout of your online store.

Online Wireframing Tools

There are several online wireframing tools available that are user-friendly and require little-to-no coding experience. Some popular options include Figma, Sketch, and Adobe XD.

eCommerce Platform

If you're using an eCommerce platform like Shopify or WooCommerce, you can use their built-in wireframing tools to create a rough layout of your online store.

Templates

Many website builders, including Wix and Squarespace, offer pre-designed templates specifically for online stores. These templates often include wireframes that you can customize to fit your needs.

In general, the easiest way to create a wireframe for an online store is to use a tool or method that you're comfortable with and that allows you to quickly and easily visualize the layout and functionality of your website.

Wireframing a Better Product Page

When wireframing a product page, there are several key considerations to keep in mind to ensure a successful user experience. Here are some points to consider:

- **Determine the layout and structure of the page:** The wireframe should outline the overall layout and structure of the page. This could include the placement of key elements such as product images, descriptions, reviews, and related products.

- **Prioritize the product image**: The product image is one of the most critical elements on the product page. The wireframe should ensure that the image is prominently displayed and optimized for quick loading times.

- **Include clear and concise product information**: The product information should be clear, concise, and highlight the key features and benefits of the product. It should be easy for users to read and understand.

- **Consider the use of videos and 360-degree images**: Videos and 360-degree images can provide users with a more immersive and detailed product experience. The wireframe should consider the placement and use of these elements.

- **Make the "add to cart" button prominent**: The "add to cart" button should be easy to find and prominently displayed on the product page. The wireframe should consider the placement and design of this button.

- **Include customer reviews and ratings**: Customer reviews and ratings can help build trust with potential customers and increase conversion rates. The wireframe should include the placement and design of these elements.

- **Optimize the page for mobile devices**: With more and more users shopping on mobile devices, the wireframe should be optimized for mobile screens. This could include using responsive design, ensuring that the site loads quickly on mobile devices, and optimizing the user interface for touch-based navigation.

Wireframing Checkout Process

Here are some best practices for UX checkout process:

Keep it simple

Your checkout process should be simple and easy to understand. Avoid unnecessary steps and fields, and try to make the process as straightforward as possible.

Use clear and concise language

Use language that is easy to understand and avoid technical terms or jargon. This will help users navigate the checkout process more easily.

Use progress indicators

Use progress indicators to show users how far they are in the checkout process and how many steps are remaining. This will help users understand what to expect and reduce anxiety.

Allow guest checkout

Allow users to checkout as a guest instead of forcing them to create an account. This will make the checkout process faster and more convenient for users who don't want to create an account.

Use auto-fill and auto-detect

Use auto-fill and auto-detect features to help users fill out forms more quickly and accurately. For example, you can automatically detect the user's location and fill in the shipping address accordingly.

Provide clear and detailed feedback

Provide users with clear and detailed feedback throughout the checkout process. This will help them understand if there are any errors or issues that need to be addressed.

Use mobile optimization

Make sure your checkout process is optimized for mobile devices. This includes using responsive design, optimizing the checkout flow for smaller screens, and using mobile-friendly input fields.

Provide multiple payment options

Provide users with multiple payment options, including credit cards, PayPal, and other popular payment methods. This will help users feel more comfortable and secure during the checkout process.

Chapter 6: Visual Design and Branding

Visual design and branding are crucial factors in creating a successful online store for several reasons.

Firstly, visual design plays a critical role in attracting and retaining customers. When visitors arrive at an online store, they will form an immediate impression based on the visual design of the website. A well-designed website with high-quality images, clear typography, and a consistent color scheme can help create a professional, trustworthy, and visually appealing online store. This can help to build trust and credibility with potential customers, which can lead to increased sales.

Secondly, branding helps to differentiate an online store from its competitors. A strong brand identity that is consistently applied across all aspects of an online store, from the logo to the website design, can help to create a unique and memorable customer experience. This can help to build brand recognition and loyalty, which can lead to increased sales and repeat business.

Thirdly, visual design and branding can help to create a cohesive and seamless customer experience. When an online store has a consistent visual design and branding, it helps customers to navigate the website more easily and find what they are looking for. This can help to reduce customer frustration and increase the likelihood of making a purchase.

Finally, visual design and branding can help to convey the personality and values of an online store. A well-designed website that reflects the brand's personality and values can help to create an emotional connection with customers, which can lead to increased customer loyalty and advocacy.

Here are more reasons why visual design is important for your online store:

- **Builds trust**: A professional and visually appealing website design can help build trust with customers, making them more likely to make a purchase.

- **Improves user experience**: A well-designed website can improve the user experience by making it easier to navigate and find products.

- **Reflects the brand's personality and values**: Visual design and branding can help communicate the personality and values of the brand, making it more relatable and appealing to customers.

- **Increases customer engagement**: A visually appealing website can increase customer engagement and encourage customers to spend more time on the website, leading to higher sales.

- **Supports marketing efforts**: Visual design and branding can support marketing efforts by providing a consistent visual identity across all marketing channels, including social media, email marketing, and advertising.

Creating a Consistent Brand Identity Through Visual Design

Creating a consistent brand identity through visual design for websites involves several key steps:

1. Establish Brand Guidelines

Start by establishing brand guidelines that define the visual identity of the brand, including colors, typography, imagery, and other design elements. These guidelines should be documented and shared with all stakeholders involved in the website design process.

2. Use Consistent Branding Elements

Use consistent branding elements throughout the website design, including logo placement, color scheme, typography, and imagery. This helps to create a cohesive and consistent visual identity that customers can easily recognize.

3. Choose A Color Palette

Choose a color palette that reflects the brand's personality and values, and use these colors consistently throughout the website. Limit the number of colors used to create a cohesive and consistent design.

4. Select Typography

Select typography that aligns with the brand's personality and values, and use these fonts consistently throughout the website. This includes font type, size, and spacing.

5. Use High-Quality Images

Use high-quality images that reflect the brand's visual identity and values. Use consistent photo styles, such as lighting, color, and composition, to create a consistent look and feel.

6. Maintain Consistency Across All Platforms

Ensure that the branding elements are consistent across all platforms, including the website, social media, and other marketing materials. This helps to reinforce the brand's identity and create a recognizable visual presence.

7. Get Feedback And Iterate

Once the website design is complete, gather feedback from stakeholders and customers to ensure that the branding elements are effective in communicating the brand's identity. Iterate as necessary to refine and improve the visual design and branding elements.

Using Color, Typography, and Imagery to Enhance the User Experience

Color, typography, and imagery are essential design elements that can significantly enhance the user experience of an online store. Here are some best practices for using these elements effectively:

1. **Color**: Color can be used to evoke emotions, convey brand personality, and guide users to important information. Some tips for using color effectively include:

    - Use a consistent color palette that reflects the brand's personality and values.
    - Use color contrast to make important information stand out, such as calls to action or product details.
    - Use colors strategically to create a hierarchy of information, with more important information using more vibrant colors.
    - Consider the cultural and psychological associations of colors to ensure they align with the brand's values and resonate with the target audience.

2. **Typography**: Typography can help communicate brand personality, convey hierarchy of information, and improve

readability. Some tips for using typography effectively include:

- Use a consistent font system that reflects the brand's personality and values.
- Use typography hierarchy to create a visual hierarchy of information, with more important information using larger font sizes and bold styles.
- Use typography contrast to make important information stand out.
- Ensure that typography is legible across different screen sizes and devices.

3. **Imagery**: Imagery can be used to create an emotional connection with the brand, showcase products, and improve the overall visual appeal of the website. Some tips for using imagery effectively include:

- Use high-quality images that reflect the brand's values and showcase the products effectively.
- Use images that resonate with the target audience and align with their interests and values.
- Use images consistently throughout the website to create a cohesive visual identity.
- Optimize images for fast loading times to improve website performance.

Designing for Different Devices and Screen Sizes

Designing for different devices and screen sizes is crucial for ensuring that the website provides a great user experience across all devices. Below are some tips for designing for different devices and screen sizes:

Use a responsive design

Responsive design is the practice of designing a website that adapts to different screen sizes and device types. This can be achieved by using a flexible grid system, flexible images, and fluid layouts that adjust to the screen size.

Use a mobile-first approach

With more users accessing websites from mobile devices, it's important to prioritize the mobile experience. A mobile-first approach involves designing the mobile version of the website first and then scaling up to larger screens. This approach ensures that the most important content is accessible on smaller screens and can help reduce load times and improve performance.

Consider the user's context

Designing for different devices also means considering the user's context. Users may be accessing the website on-the-go, in different locations, and with varying levels of attention. Designing with these factors in mind can help create a user-friendly experience that meets the user's needs.

Test across devices and screen sizes

It's important to test the website across different devices and screen sizes to ensure that the design is responsive and provides a good user experience. There are various tools available for testing the website on different devices, including emulators and real device testing.

Prioritize content and functionality

When designing for different devices, it's important to prioritize content and functionality. This means designing for the most important tasks and information first, and then adding additional features and content as screen size increases.

Ensuring Accessibility and Responsive Design

Ensuring accessibility and responsive design for an online store is essential to provide a positive user experience for all users, regardless of their device or abilities.

Best Practices for Accessibility and Responsive Design for an Online Store:

- **Use semantic HTML**: Use semantic HTML to ensure that screen readers can easily navigate the website and that content is structured in a logical and organized manner.

- **Add alt tags to images**: Alt tags provide a text description of images for users who are visually impaired or have images disabled. This ensures that all users can understand the content of the website.

- **Ensure high color contrast**: Ensure that text has high color contrast with its background, making it easier for users with color blindness or visual impairments to read.

- **Use clear and readable fonts**: Use fonts that are easy to read, even at smaller sizes. Avoid fancy fonts or fonts with low contrast.

- **Ensure keyboard accessibility**: Ensure that the website can be navigated using only a keyboard, as some users may not be able to use a mouse.

- **Test for accessibility:** Test the website for accessibility using tools such as screen readers, keyboard-only navigation, and color contrast checkers. Get feedback from users with disabilities to ensure that the website is accessible and easy to use.

Ensuring accessibility and responsive design for an online store involves using semantic HTML, adding alt tags to images, ensuring high color contrast, using clear and readable fonts, ensuring keyboard accessibility, using responsive design, and testing for accessibility.

Designing a Better Home Page

When designing the home page of an online store, there are several best practices to consider.

Keep it simple and clean

The home page design should be simple and clean, with a clear hierarchy of information. Avoid cluttered designs that overwhelm users with too much information.

Use high-quality images

High-quality images can help create a visually appealing home page that draws users in. Choose images that are relevant to your products and brand.

Showcase featured products

Consider showcasing featured products or promotions on the homepage to help drive sales and increase engagement.

Include customer reviews and ratings

Including customer reviews and ratings on the home page can help build trust with potential customers and increase conversion rates.

Use clear calls to action

Use clear calls to action (CTAs) to encourage users to take specific actions, such as signing up for a newsletter or making a purchase. Use contrasting colors and placement to make the CTAs stand out.

Use social proof

Consider including social proof elements such as customer testimonials, awards, and trust badges to help build credibility and trust with potential customers.

Use analytics to inform design decisions

Use analytics to track user behavior and make data-driven design decisions. This can help you optimize the home page design for better engagement and sales.

By following these best practices, you can design a homepage that is visually appealing, easy to navigate, and optimized for engagement and sales.

Designing a Better Product Page

When designing a product page for an online store, there are several key visual design considerations to keep in mind.

Use high-quality product images

High-quality product images are essential for any product page. They should be clear, well-lit, and showcase the product from different angles. The images should also be optimized for fast loading times.

Create visual hierarchy

The design should create a visual hierarchy that guides the user's attention to the most important elements on the page. This could include the product image, product title, price, and "add to cart" button.

Use whitespace effectively

Whitespace can help create a clean and organized design that is easy to read and navigate. The wireframe should consider the use of whitespace to help guide the user's attention and make the page more visually appealing.

Use contrasting colors for key elements

Contrasting colors can help draw the user's attention to key elements on the page, such as the "add to cart" button. The wireframe should consider the use of color to help create visual contrast and make the page more engaging.

Use typography effectively

Typography can help create a consistent visual style and improve readability. The wireframe should consider the use of typography to make the product information more clear and easy to read.

Consider the use of multimedia

Multimedia elements such as videos, animations, and interactive images can help create a more engaging product page. The wireframe should consider the placement and use of these elements.

Optimize the design for mobile devices

With more and more users shopping on mobile devices, the wireframe should be optimized for mobile screens. This could include using responsive design, ensuring that the site loads quickly on mobile devices, and optimizing the user interface for touch-based navigation.

By considering these key visual design considerations, you can create a visually engaging product page that helps increase user engagement and conversion rates.

Chapter 7: Prototyping

Prototyping is important when developing an online store because it allows designers and developers to test and refine the user experience before the website is launched. A prototype is a simplified version of the website that allows users to interact with the site and provide feedback on the design, functionality, and overall user experience.

There are several reasons why prototyping is important when developing an online store. First, it allows designers and developers to test the usability of the website and identify any issues or areas for improvement. By testing the website with real users, designers and developers can gain valuable insights into how users interact with the site, what they find confusing or frustrating, and what they like about the design.

Second, prototyping allows designers and developers to test the functionality of the website. By simulating the user experience and testing different scenarios, designers and developers can identify any bugs or technical issues that need to be addressed before the website is launched.

Third, prototyping allows designers and developers to iterate on the design and refine the user experience. By testing different design options and gathering feedback from users, designers and developers can make informed decisions about the design and user experience that will ultimately lead to a better online store.

Finally, prototyping can save time and money in the long run by identifying and addressing issues early in the development process. By catching issues before the website is launched, designers and developers can avoid costly and time-consuming fixes after the site has gone live.

When prototyping an online store, there are several factors that you should consider to ensure that your prototype is effective and successful:

- **User experience**: The user experience is crucial for any online store. Your prototype should focus on providing a seamless and intuitive user experience for visitors to your site.

- **Design and branding**: The design and branding of your online store should be consistent and aligned with your brand identity. Ensure that the prototype reflects your brand's personality and tone.

- **Navigation**: The navigation of your online store should be easy to use and intuitive. Ensure that the prototype includes all necessary pages, categories, and links.

- **Product information:** Your prototype should include accurate and detailed product information, including images, descriptions, and pricing.

- **Analytics**: If possible, your prototype should include analytics tracking so that you can monitor user behavior and make data-driven decisions.

Tools for Prototyping

There are several tools available for online store prototyping. Here are some of the best:

- **Adobe Figma**: Figma is a web-based design tool that allows for collaboration and real-time feedback. It's great for prototyping online stores as it has a wide range of design elements and templates.

- **Adobe XD**: Adobe XD is another popular design tool for prototyping online stores. It's easy to use and has a variety of features that allow for the creation of interactive prototypes.

- **Sketch**: Sketch is a vector-based design tool that is ideal for prototyping online stores. It has a large library of plugins and templates, making it easy to create designs quickly.

- **InVision**: InVision is a prototyping and collaboration tool that allows for the creation of interactive online store prototypes. It has a variety of features that make it easy to share designs and get feedback.

- **Marvel**: Marvel is a web-based prototyping tool that is easy to use and allows for the creation of interactive prototypes for online stores.

- **Axure**: Axure is a prototyping tool that is ideal for creating complex online store prototypes. It has a variety of features that allow for the creation of interactive designs, including animations and dynamic content.

These are just a few of the best tools for online store prototyping. Ultimately, the best tool for you will depend on your specific needs and preferences.

Chapter 8: Usability Testing

Usability testing is an important tool for online stores to improve their user experience and ultimately sell more. Usability testing involves observing real users interacting with the website to identify any issues or areas for improvement in the design, functionality, and overall user experience.

Steps you can follow to conduct a usability test for an online store

1. Define your Testing Goals

The first step is to define your testing goals. Identify what you want to learn from the usability test, such as whether users can navigate the site, find what they're looking for, and complete the checkout process.

2. Recruit Participants

Recruit participants who fit your target audience. You can use a recruitment agency, social media, or email list to find participants.

3. Develop Tasks

Create tasks that simulate real-world scenarios that users would encounter on your online store. For example, ask participants to find a specific product, add it to their cart, and checkout.

4. Conduct the Test

Use a screen recording tool to capture participants' interactions with your online store while they complete the tasks you've assigned. Encourage participants to think aloud and share their thoughts and feelings as they navigate your site.

5. Analyze the Results

Review the screen recordings and identify any usability issues that participants encountered. Look for patterns and themes in the feedback, and prioritize the most critical issues that need to be addressed.

6. Iterate and Improve

Use the feedback from the usability test to make improvements to your online store. Implement changes and test again to see if the improvements have resolved any usability issues.

In addition to the above steps, it's important to consider the following best practices for usability testing:

- **Test early and often**: Conduct usability testing throughout the design process to catch issues early and prevent costly redesigns.

- **Use a diverse set of participants**: Ensure that you test with a diverse set of participants to get a wide range of feedback.

- **Keep it realistic:** Use realistic scenarios and tasks that simulate what users would actually encounter on your online store.

- **Make it easy for participants**: Ensure that the testing process is easy for participants by providing clear instructions and minimizing distractions.

- **Focus on actionable feedback**: Look for feedback that is actionable and can be used to make improvements to your online store.

Using A/B testing to optimize conversion rates and sales

A/B testing, also known as split testing, is a method of comparing two versions of a webpage to determine which one performs better. Here are some steps to use A/B testing to optimize conversion rates and sales for your online store:

TAKE ACTION
Creating A/B tests
1. Identify the areas to tes
2. Develop your hypotheses
3. Create your variations
4. Test your variations
5. Analyze your results
6. Iterate and repeat

1. Identify the areas to test

Start by identifying the areas of your online store that you want to test. This could be the layout of your product pages, the copy on your call-to-action buttons, or the placement of your navigation menu.

2. Develop your hypotheses

Based on your observations and research, develop a hypothesis about which version of the webpage will perform better. For example, you may hypothesize that changing the color of your call-to-action button from blue to red will increase click-through rates.

3. Create your variations

Create two versions of your webpage: the control version and the variation. The control version should be the original version of the webpage, while the variation should include the changes you want to test.

4. Test your variations

Use an A/B testing tool to randomly show each visitor either the control version or the variation. Measure the performance of each version by tracking the conversion rates, bounce rates, and other relevant metrics.

5. Analyze your results

Once you have enough data, analyze the results of your A/B test to determine which version performed better. If the variation outperforms the control, you can make it the new control version and test new variations.

6. Iterate and repeat

A/B testing should be an ongoing process, so continue to identify areas for improvement and test new variations to optimize your conversion rates and sales.

Continuously iterating and improving UX design based on user feedback

Continuously iterating and improving UX design based on user feedback is a good thing for an online store for several reasons:

Better user experience

When you continuously iterate and improve the UX design of your online store based on user feedback, you create a better user experience. This can lead to increased engagement, higher conversion rates, and greater customer satisfaction.

Competitive advantage

By constantly improving the UX design of your online store, you can stay ahead of your competitors. If your competitors are not putting as much effort into UX design, you can gain a competitive advantage by providing a better user experience.

Increased loyalty

When customers have a positive experience on your online store, they are more likely to return and make repeat purchases. Continuously improving your UX design can help increase customer loyalty and retention.

Better insights into user behavior

User feedback can provide valuable insights into how users interact with your online store. By continuously analyzing and acting on this feedback, you can gain a better understanding of user behavior and preferences.

Cost-effective

Making small, incremental improvements to your UX design based on user feedback can be more cost-effective than overhauling your entire online store design at once. This allows you to make improvements over time without breaking the bank.

Overall, continuously iterating and improving UX design based on user feedback is a good thing for an online store as it can lead to better user experiences, increased loyalty, and a competitive advantage.

Heuristic Analysis

Heuristic analysis is a method of evaluating the user interface design of a website or application based on a set of established usability principles. Below is a general process for performing a heuristic analysis of an online store:

1. **Define the usability principles**: Identify a set of usability principles to use as the basis for your analysis. The most common set of principles used for heuristic analysis is Nielsen's 10 usability heuristics.

2. **Evaluate the website**: Go through the website systematically, page by page, and evaluate the user interface design against each of the usability principles. Use a checklist to keep track of your findings.

3. **Identify usability issues**: As you evaluate the website, identify any usability issues that violate the usability principles. Be specific and provide examples of the issue, such as confusing navigation, unclear labels, or slow page load times.

4. **Categorize issues by severity**: Categorize the usability issues you've identified by severity, from high to low. High severity issues are those that are likely to have the biggest

impact on user experience and should be addressed as a priority.

5. **Prioritize issues for improvement:** Based on the severity of the usability issues, prioritize which ones should be addressed first. Consider the impact on user experience, the frequency of the issue, and the effort required to fix it.

6. **Provide recommendations**: For each usability issue identified, provide specific recommendations for improvement. Be specific and provide examples of how the issue can be addressed.

7. **Summarize findings**: Summarize your findings in a report or presentation, highlighting the most significant usability issues and recommendations for improvement.

Nielsen's 10 Usability Heuristics

Nielsen's 10 usability heuristics are a set of principles that are commonly used in heuristic evaluation to assess the user experience design of a website or application. These heuristics were developed by Jakob Nielsen and Rolf Molich in the 1990s and have since been widely adopted as a standard for evaluating user interface design. Here are the 10 heuristics:

1. **Visibility of system status:** The system should always keep users informed about what is going on, through appropriate feedback within a reasonable amount of time.

2. **Match between system and the real world**: The system should speak the users' language, with words, phrases and concepts familiar to the user, rather than system-oriented terms. Follow real-world conventions, making information appear in a natural and logical order.

3. **User control and freedom**: Users often make mistakes, so the system should allow users to undo or reverse their actions. The system should also offer clear and easy-to-find exit points.

4. **Consistency and standards**: Users should not have to wonder whether different words, situations, or actions mean the same thing. Follow platform conventions.

5. **Error prevention**: Even better than good error messages is a careful design which prevents a problem from occurring in the first place. Either eliminate error-prone conditions or check for them and present users with a confirmation option before they commit to the action.

6. **Recognition rather than recall**: Minimize the user's memory load by making objects, actions, and options visible. The user should not have to remember information from one part of the interface to another. Instructions for use of the system should be visible or easily retrievable whenever appropriate.

7. **Flexibility and efficiency of use**: Shortcuts, accelerators, and other efficiency-focused tools should be provided so that expert users can save time on common actions.

8. **Aesthetic and minimalist design**: Dialogues should not contain information which is irrelevant or rarely needed. Every extra unit of information in a dialogue competes with the relevant units of information and diminishes their relative visibility.

9. **Help users recognize, diagnose, and recover from errors**: Error messages should be expressed in plain language (no codes), precisely indicate the problem, and constructively suggest a solution.

10. **Help and documentation**: Even though it is better if the system can be used without documentation, it may be necessary to provide help and documentation. Any such information should be easy to search, focused on the user's task, list concrete steps to be carried out, and not be too large.

Usability Test Online Tools

UserTesting
Allows you to test your website, app, or prototype with real users. You can choose your target audience and receive video recordings of their interaction and feedback.

TryMyUI
Offers remote user testing to improve website and app usability. It provides video recordings of testers using your product, along with written feedback and suggestions.

UserZoom
Offers various usability testing methods, such as card sorting, surveys, and remote user testing. It provides detailed reports with quantitative and qualitative data.

Optimal Workshop
Offers a suite of tools for user research and design, including card sorting, tree testing, and first-click testing. It helps you understand how users navigate and interact with your site or app.

Maze

Maze offers user testing and research tools to improve product design. It allows you to create and run usability tests and collect feedback from users in real-time.

Lookback

Lookback is a user research platform that offers moderated and unmoderated user testing, as well as analytics and insights. It enables you to record and analyze user interactions on your website or app.

Validately

Validately offers remote moderated and unmoderated usability testing, as well as survey and feedback tools. It provides video recordings of testers interacting with your product, along with detailed reports.

Userlytics

Offers user testing and research tools, including remote usability testing, card sorting, and survey tools. It provides video recordings of testers using your product, along with written feedback and suggestions.

These are just a few examples of usability testing online tools available. There are many others, so it's worth researching and trying out a few to find the one that works best for your needs.

Common usability mistakes that online stores often make:

1. **Poor Navigation**: If users can't find what they're looking for quickly and easily, they'll likely abandon the site. Poor navigation can include unclear categories, hidden menus, or

confusing labeling.

2. **Cluttered or Complex Layout**: A cluttered or complex layout can make it difficult for users to understand what they should do next or where they should go to find what they need. Online stores should strive for a clean, simple, and intuitive design.

3. **Inconsistent Design**: Inconsistent design elements can create confusion and lead to a disjointed user experience. For example, inconsistent colors, fonts, and button styles can make it difficult for users to understand the site's hierarchy.

4. **Long Checkout Process:** A long and complicated checkout process can lead to cart abandonment. It's essential to keep the checkout process as simple and streamlined as possible.

5. **Poor Product Descriptions and Images**: Users rely on product descriptions and images to make informed purchase decisions. Poor or insufficient product information can lead to frustration and lost sales.

Avoid these common usability mistakes to improve the user experience and increase sales.

Chapter 9: Interaction Design and User Interface (UI)

Interaction design and user interface (UI) are essential elements in creating an effective and engaging online store. Below are some key considerations for creating an effective interaction design and UI:

Understand user needs

It's essential to understand the needs and preferences of your target audience to create an interaction design and UI that resonates with them. Conduct user research and analysis to gain insights into your users' behavior, preferences, and pain points.

Create a user-friendly interface

A user-friendly interface is essential for enhancing the user experience of an online store. Ensure that the design is easy to navigate and visually appealing. Use a clear hierarchy of information and intuitive navigation to help users find what they need quickly.

Use a consistent design language

Consistency is key to creating a memorable brand and user experience. Use consistent branding, typography, color schemes, and imagery throughout the online store to create a cohesive user experience.

Use microinteractions

Microinteractions are small interactions that occur within the UI and help users complete tasks quickly and easily. Use microinteractions such as tooltips, hover states, and progress indicators to improve the user experience of the online store.

Designing interactive elements that enhance the user experience

Designing interactive elements can help enhance the user experience for an online store and increase engagement. Here are some tips for designing interactive elements:

Use animations and transitions

Animations and transitions can help provide feedback to users and create a more dynamic user experience. Use them sparingly to avoid overwhelming the user, but strategically to enhance the user experience.

Create interactive product showcases

Interactive product showcases, such as 360-degree product views or product videos, can help users understand the product better and increase their confidence in making a purchase.

Use interactive forms and surveys

Interactive forms and surveys can help users provide feedback and input more easily. Use them to collect user data, feedback, and preferences.

Incorporate gamification

Gamification elements, such as quizzes, challenges, or rewards, can help increase user engagement and create a more fun and interactive user experience.

Include social proof elements

Social proof elements, such as customer reviews, ratings, and testimonials, can help build trust with users and increase their confidence in making a purchase.

Test and iterate

Test your interactive elements with real users to gather feedback and make improvements. Continuously iterate and refine your interactive elements to enhance the user experience and achieve business goals.

Using UI patterns and conventions for familiarity and ease of use

Using UI patterns and conventions can help create a familiar and easy-to-use user interface for an online store. Here are some tips for using UI patterns and conventions:

Use familiar UI elements

Use common UI elements that users are already familiar with, such as navigation menus, search bars, and buttons. This can help users quickly understand how to interact with your website.

Follow established design patterns

Use established design patterns, such as card layouts, sliders, and accordions, to create a consistent and familiar user interface.

Stick to common design conventions

Stick to common design conventions, such as using a hamburger menu icon for mobile navigation or placing the logo in the top left corner, to create a consistent and familiar user interface.

Keep it simple

Avoid using too many different UI patterns and conventions, as this can lead to confusion and overwhelm users. Keep it simple and use only the most relevant UI patterns and conventions for your online store.

Using UI patterns and conventions involves using familiar UI elements, following established design patterns, sticking to common design conventions, keeping it simple, and testing and iterating. By using UI patterns and conventions, you can create a user interface that is familiar, easy to use, and helps users quickly understand how to interact with your online store.

Incorporating user feedback to improve UI design

Incorporating user feedback is an important part of improving UI design for an online store.

Tips on how to do this effectively:

1. **Collect feedback**: Collect feedback from your users through surveys, user testing, and social media. You can also use tools like Hotjar or UserTesting to collect feedback and insights about your website.

2. **Analyze feedback**: Analyze the feedback you receive to identify common issues and areas for improvement. Look for patterns in the feedback and prioritize the issues that have the biggest impact on the user experience.

3. **Make changes**: Use the feedback you've collected to make changes to your UI design. This could involve making adjustments to the layout, navigation, or visual design of your website.

4. **Test changes**: Test the changes you've made with real users to see how they respond. You can use A/B testing to compare the effectiveness of different UI designs and identify which changes are most effective.

5. **Repeat**: Continuously iterate and improve your UI design based on the feedback you receive. Use a feedback loop to constantly gather feedback, make changes, and test those changes with real users.

By incorporating user feedback into your UI design process, you can create a user interface that is more effective, engaging, and easy to use. This will help improve the overall user experience of your online store, leading to increased user satisfaction, engagement, and sales.

Chapter 10: UX and Customer Service

Customer service is part of the user experience of an online store, and it is very important because it directly affects how customers interact with the website and how they perceive the brand. Below are some of the reasons why UX is important to customer service:

Brand perception

The user experience on a website can directly impact how customers perceive the brand. A positive user experience can increase trust and credibility, while a negative user experience can lead to frustration and distrust.

Reduced support needs

By providing a good user experience, online stores can reduce the volume of customer service inquiries. This allows customer service representatives to focus on more complex issues, which can lead to faster response times and increased customer satisfaction.

Improved customer satisfaction

A good user experience can improve customer satisfaction by making it easier for customers to complete their transactions and find the information they need. This can lead to increased loyalty and repeat business.

Increased sales

By providing a positive user experience, online stores can increase the likelihood that customers will complete their purchases. This can lead to increased sales and revenue for the business.

Improve your Customer Service with UX

UX, or user experience, can greatly help the customer service of an online store by making it easier for customers to navigate the website, find the information they need, and complete their transactions. Here are some ways UX can improve customer service:

1. **Offer multiple channels for communication**: Provide multiple channels for customers to reach out to you such as email, live chat, phone, and social media. Make sure to respond promptly to customer inquiries through these channels.

2. **Have a clear return policy**: Clearly state your return policy and make it easy for customers to initiate a return or exchange. Consider offering free returns or exchanges to improve customer satisfaction.

3. **Provide detailed product information**: Ensure that your product descriptions are detailed and accurate. Include information such as dimensions, materials, and care instructions to help customers make informed purchasing decisions.

4. **Offer proactive customer support**: Be proactive in addressing customer concerns by reaching out to them before they reach out to you. For example, you can send a follow-up email after a purchase to ensure that the customer is satisfied with their purchase.

5. **Provide personalized service**: Personalize the customer experience by using the customer's name and offering personalized recommendations based on their previous purchases or browsing history.

6. **Respond to customer feedback**: Respond to customer feedback promptly and take action to address any issues or concerns they may have.

Self-service support

Providing customers with self-service support options, such as an FAQ page or a knowledge base, can help reduce the volume of customer service inquiries. This allows customer service representatives to focus on more complex issues. Self-service support for an online store refers to a set of resources that customers can access on their own to find solutions to their problems or answers to their questions, without having to contact customer support. These resources typically include:

- **Frequently asked questions (FAQs)**: This section of the website provides answers to common questions that customers may have, such as shipping and return policies, payment methods, product specifications, and more.

- **Knowledge base:** A knowledge base is a database of information about a product or service, including how-tos, troubleshooting guides, and other instructional content. It provides customers with step-by-step guidance to solve their problems.

- **Chatbots**: Some online stores use chatbots to provide quick and automated support to customers. These chatbots are designed to answer common questions and provide solutions to common problems.

Chapter 11: Upselling and Cross-selling

Upselling is a powerful strategy that online stores can use to increase their revenue and customer loyalty. Effective upselling can lead to higher average order values, resulting in increased profits. Personalization is key to successful upselling, as it allows stores to make relevant product recommendations based on customer data. By using customer segmentation, stores can tailor their recommendations to different customer groups, making the upsell more compelling.

To be effective, the upsell must **provide clear value** to the customer. Stores should highlight the benefits of the product and explain how it will meet the customer's needs. A good example of this would be suggesting an upsell for a faster processor or more storage space for a laptop, and explaining how this will improve the customer's user experience. Pricing is also important, and stores should ensure that the upsell offers value for money.

Finally, **timing is critical** when it comes to upselling. Stores should present the upsell at the right moment, such as after the customer has added an item to their cart or during the checkout process. Bombarding customers with too many upsell offers can be overwhelming and counterproductive.

Upselling and cross-selling are effective strategies for increasing the average order value and revenue of an online store. When done correctly, upselling and cross-selling can actually improve the user experience (UX) for customers. Here are some of the best strategies for implementing these techniques:

Personalization

Use customer data to personalize product recommendations based on their browsing and purchase history. This can make the recommendations more relevant to the customer and increase the likelihood of a purchase.

Product Bundling

Offer product bundles that combine complementary items at a discounted price. This can encourage customers to purchase more items and increase the average order value.

Related Product Recommendations

Provide related product recommendations on product pages or during checkout. This can suggest products that complement the items in the customer's cart and increase the likelihood of an upsell or cross-sell.

Limited-Time Offers

Use limited-time offers or discounts to incentivize customers to purchase additional items. This can create a sense of urgency and encourage customers to take advantage of the offer.

Post-Purchase Follow-Up

Send follow-up emails or notifications after a purchase to suggest complementary or related products. This can encourage repeat purchases and increase the lifetime value of the customer.

Improved Product Discovery

Upselling and cross-selling can help customers discover new products that they may not have otherwise known about. This can provide a more engaging and exploratory shopping experience, which can be more enjoyable for customers.

Enhanced Value Proposition

By offering discounts or bundling products together, online stores can communicate the value proposition of their products more clearly. This can help customers understand the benefits of purchasing additional items and make it easier for them to justify the added expense.

Using upselling and cross-selling techniques in a strategic and customer-focused way, online stores can improve the user experience and help customers find products that meet their needs. This can lead to increased customer satisfaction, loyalty, and revenue for the business.

Chapter 12: Measuring Success and ROI

Measuring success and return on investment (ROI) is important for an online store for several reasons:

Identify areas for improvement

Measuring success and ROI can help you identify areas of your online store that are performing well and areas that need improvement. This information can guide future investments and improvements to the site.

Determine the effectiveness of marketing efforts

Measuring success and ROI can help you determine the effectiveness of your marketing efforts. This can help you identify which marketing channels are driving the most traffic and sales, and where to invest more resources.

Track progress towards goals

Measuring success and ROI can help you track your progress towards business goals such as revenue, profit, and customer acquisition. This can help you stay on track and adjust strategies as needed.

Make data-driven decisions

Measuring success and ROI provides valuable data that can inform future decisions related to the online store. This can help you make more informed, data-driven decisions that are likely to lead to better results.

Justify investments

Measuring success and ROI can help you justify investments in the online store to stakeholders such as investors, partners, and employees. This can help ensure ongoing support and resources for the site.

Overall, measuring success and ROI is important for an online store because it helps identify areas for improvement, determine the effectiveness of marketing efforts, track progress towards goals, make data-driven decisions, and justify investments.

Defining metrics for measuring the success of UX improvements

Defining metrics for measuring the success of UX improvements for an online store involves identifying specific goals and objectives, and selecting metrics that align with those goals. Here are some steps to follow:

Identify goals and objectives

Start by identifying the specific goals and objectives you want to achieve through UX improvements. For example, you may want to increase conversions, reduce cart abandonment rates, or improve customer satisfaction.

Determine key performance indicators (KPIs)

Once you have identified your goals and objectives, determine the key performance indicators (KPIs) that will help you measure progress towards those goals. For example, if your goal is to increase conversions, a KPI may be the conversion rate.

Choose metrics

Once you have identified KPIs, select specific metrics that align with those KPIs. For example, if your KPI is conversion rate, specific metrics may include the number of completed transactions, average order value, and customer lifetime value.

Set targets

Set targets for each metric based on your goals and objectives. For example, if your goal is to increase conversions, you may set a target to increase conversion rates by 10% within the next six months.

Monitor and analyze data

Once you have set targets, monitor and analyze data to track progress towards your goals. Use data analytics tools to track metrics, identify trends, and gain insights that can help guide future improvements.

By following these steps, you can define metrics for measuring the success of UX improvements for your online store and use data-driven insights to continuously improve the user experience.

Key Performance Indicators (KPIs) and their Importance for Online Stores

KPI stands for Key Performance Indicators. These are measurable metrics that businesses use to track and evaluate their performance over time. KPIs help organizations set objectives, monitor progress, and make data-driven decisions. The KPIs that a business tracks will depend on its specific goals and objectives, but some common examples include website traffic, conversion rates, customer acquisition cost, and revenue growth. By regularly tracking and analyzing KPIs, businesses can identify areas for improvement and make adjustments to their strategies to optimize their performance.

For an online store, KPIs are particularly important because they can help measure the success of various marketing and sales strategies. For example, tracking website traffic can help determine the effectiveness of SEO efforts, while monitoring conversion rates can provide insights into the performance of product pages and checkout processes. By measuring KPIs related to customer acquisition and retention, businesses can gain a better understanding of their target audience and how to effectively engage and retain them. Ultimately, tracking KPIs can help online stores make data-driven decisions that drive growth and improve overall performance.

Here are some of the most common KPIs to analyze and improve an online store:

1. **Conversion Rate**: The percentage of visitors who complete a desired action, such as making a purchase or filling out a form.

2. **Traffic Sources**: The channels through which visitors are finding your site, such as search engines, social media, or referrals.

3. **Average Order Value (AOV)**: The average amount of money customers spend per order.

4. **Cart Abandonment Rate**: The percentage of visitors who add items to their cart but do not complete the checkout process.

5. **Customer Lifetime Value (CLV)**: The total amount of revenue a customer is expected to generate over their lifetime.

6. **Return on Ad Spend (ROAS)**: The revenue generated by advertising campaigns compared to the cost of the campaigns.

7. **Customer Satisfaction (CSAT)**: A metric that measures how satisfied customers are with their overall shopping experience.

8. **Net Promoter Score (NPS)**: A metric that measures how

likely customers are to recommend your store to others.

9. **Website Speed:** The time it takes for your website to load, which can affect user experience and search engine rankings.

10. **Bounce Rate**: The percentage of visitors who leave your site after viewing only one page.

Monitoring KPIs can help businesses improve the UX of their website by identifying areas for improvement and making data-driven decisions to optimize it. By improving the UX, businesses can increase engagement, drive conversions, and ultimately improve their bottom line.

Chapter 13: Why investing in UX is a good strategy for an online store?

Investing in UX is the best strategy for an online store because it directly impacts the user experience, which is crucial in driving sales and building brand loyalty. A well-designed user experience can create a positive impression of the online store, making it easier for customers to navigate the site, find what they're looking for, and complete their purchases. By investing in UX, online stores can create a seamless user experience that builds trust and encourages customers to return. Additionally, a good UX can differentiate an online store from its competitors, making it more likely to attract new customers and retain existing ones. Overall, investing in UX is a smart strategy that can help drive sales and build a successful online store.

Investing in UX is the best strategy to improve sales of an online store for several reasons:

Better User Experience

A well-designed UX can improve the overall user experience, making it easier for customers to find products, make purchases, and engage with your brand. By providing a positive user experience, you can increase customer satisfaction, loyalty, and ultimately drive more sales.

Increased Conversion Rates

By optimizing the UX for conversion, you can increase the likelihood that customers will make a purchase. A well-designed UX can reduce friction, eliminate distractions, and provide a clear path to purchase, leading to increased conversion rates.

Competitive Advantage

With so many online stores competing for customers' attention, a well-designed UX can provide a competitive advantage. By providing a better user experience than your competitors, you can stand out and attract more customers.

Reduced Abandonment Rates

Abandoned carts are a common problem for online stores, but a well-designed UX can help reduce abandonment rates. By simplifying the checkout process, providing clear calls to action, and reducing friction, you can increase the likelihood that customers will complete their purchase.

Improved Brand Perception

A positive user experience can improve customers' perception of your brand, leading to increased loyalty and repeat business. By investing in UX, you're investing in the long-term success of your brand.

Good User Experience Increases Retention

Retention is crucial for the success of ecommerce businesses. With a vast array of online stores available to consumers, retaining existing customers is vital to maintaining a competitive edge. Loyal customers are more likely to return to a website, make repeat purchases, and recommend products or services to their friends and family. As a result, they can drive significant revenue growth for ecommerce businesses.

Furthermore, retention is more cost-effective than acquisition. Acquiring new customers can be expensive, particularly through paid advertising channels. By retaining existing customers, ecommerce businesses can reduce their customer acquisition costs and improve their overall return on investment. This is particularly important for startups and small businesses, who may not have the budget to invest in costly acquisition strategies.

Finally, customer retention is also key to improving the overall customer experience. Ecommerce businesses that focus on retention can offer personalized recommendations, loyalty programs, and other retention tactics that enhance the customer experience. By creating a positive experience, customers are more likely to return to a website and make additional purchases, leading to increased revenue and profitability over time.

In conclusion, retention is crucial to the success of ecommerce businesses. By focusing on strategies to retain customers, such as loyalty programs and personalized recommendations, businesses can improve customer satisfaction, reduce acquisition costs, and drive revenue growth. With so many online stores available to consumers, retention is a critical differentiator that can help businesses stand out in a competitive market.

Conclusion

Investing in UX is the best strategy to improve sales of an online store because it enhances the user experience, increases conversion rates, provides a competitive advantage, reduces abandonment rates, and improves brand perception. By focusing on the user experience, you can create a better online shopping experience for your customers and ultimately drive more sales and revenue for your business.

Chapter 14: Summary and Future Trends

Summarizing the Importance Of UX Design in Online Stores

In summary, UX design is crucial for the success of online stores as it ensures that the website is easy to use, visually appealing, and engaging to users. Through user research, analysis, and testing, UX designers can identify user needs, pain points, and behaviors to inform design decisions that improve the user experience. By creating intuitive navigation, accessible and responsive design, and consistent branding, online stores can build trust and loyalty with their customers.

Continuous iteration and improvement based on user feedback and data can result in increased conversion rates and ROI. It is essential to communicate the value of UX design to stakeholders and decision-makers to ensure that resources are allocated appropriately to achieve business goals.

Does UX solely revolve around testing?

User experience (UX) is not solely about testing and analysis, but it is a significant aspect of it. UX is a broad field that encompasses many different disciplines, including design, research, psychology, and engineering. Testing and analysis are essential components of the UX process because they help to ensure that a product or service meets the needs and expectations of its users.

UX testing involves evaluating a product or service by observing how users interact with it. This can include conducting user surveys, usability testing, A/B testing, and other forms of user research.

Analysis involves analyzing the data collected from these tests and using it to make data-driven decisions to improve the UX.

However, UX is more than just testing and analysis. It also involves understanding the needs and goals of users and designing products and services that meet those needs. This involves empathy, creativity, and collaboration across different disciplines. UX designers must be able to communicate effectively with other team members, including developers and stakeholders, to create products and services that are functional, usable, and enjoyable for users.

Identifying Best Practices for Improving the User Experience in Online Stores

Here are some best practices for improving the user experience in online stores:

1. Conduct user research and analysis to understand user needs and behaviors.
2. Create intuitive and easy-to-use navigation to help users find what they're looking for.
3. Ensure your website is accessible and responsive on all devices.
4. Use clear and concise copy to communicate product information and benefits.
5. Use high-quality product images and videos to showcase products.
6. Implement a consistent visual design and branding across the website.
7. Provide relevant and helpful product recommendations and search results.
8. Use interactive elements such as product configurators, chatbots, and personalized recommendations.

9. Optimize website speed and performance for faster loading times.
10. Use A/B testing and other analytics tools to evaluate the effectiveness of design changes and make data-driven decisions.

Exploring Emerging UX Design Trends and Technologies

As a language model, I can provide some insights into the emerging UX design trends and technologies that are currently shaping the industry. Here are some of the most notable ones:

Voice Interfaces

With the rise of smart speakers and virtual assistants, voice interfaces are becoming more prevalent in UX design. Designers need to consider the unique challenges and opportunities presented by voice interfaces, such as natural language processing, tone, and pacing.

Augmented Reality

Augmented reality (AR) technology is being integrated into UX design to create more immersive and engaging experiences. AR can be used to enhance product visualizations, improve user onboarding, and create more interactive content.

AI and Machine Learning

Artificial intelligence (AI) and machine learning are transforming UX design by enabling more personalized and contextually relevant experiences. Designers can use AI to analyze user behavior, personalize content, and automate processes to enhance the user experience.

Dark Mode

Dark mode is a design trend that has gained popularity over the last few years. This feature provides a high-contrast, dark color scheme that can be easier on the eyes in low-light environments, conserve battery life on mobile devices, and create a sleek, modern aesthetic.

3D Graphics

3D graphics are being used to create more visually stunning and engaging interfaces. This technology allows designers to create realistic, interactive objects and environments that can be manipulated by users.

Microinteractions

Microinteractions are small, subtle animations or feedback loops that enhance the user experience. These tiny interactions can be used to provide visual feedback, create a sense of delight, or guide users through complex processes.

Progressive Web Apps

Progressive web apps (PWAs) are web applications that provide a mobile app-like experience. PWAs are designed to be fast, responsive, and work seamlessly on any device or platform, making them an attractive alternative to traditional mobile apps.

Overall, UX design is continually evolving, and keeping up with emerging trends and technologies is essential for designers to create engaging and innovative experiences for users.

www.ingramcontent.com/pod-product-compliance
Lightning Source LLC
LaVergne TN
LVHW051709050326
832903LV00032B/4093